First Comes Love

All About the Birds and the Bees— and Alligators, Possums, and People, Too

By Jennifer Davis
Illustrated by Clare Mackie

WORKMAN PUBLISHING • NEW YORK

For Jill, who keeps enough love, joy, and
pizzazz in her pocket to share with everyone
who knows her. And for Henry, Liza, Lily, and
Jack, who, like their grandmother,
fill my house with laughter.

—JD

For my friends.

—CM

The author is grateful for permission to reprint an excerpt from LET'S DO IT, by Cole Porter, © 1928 (Renewed) Warner Bros. Inc.,
All Rights Reserved. Used by permission, WARNER BROS. PUBLICATIONS U.S. INC. Miami, FL. 33014.

Library of Congress Cataloging-in-Publication Data
Davis, Jennifer, 1956–
First comes love : all about the birds and the bees—and alligators, possums, and people, too / by Jennifer Davis ; illustrated by Clare Mackie.
p. cm.
ISBN 0-7611-2244-3
1. Courtship of animals—Juvenile literature. 2. Reproduction—Juvenile literature.
[1.Animals—Courtship. 2. Animals—Habits and behavior. 3. Reproduction.] I. Mackie, Clare, ill. II. Title.
QL761.D38 2001   591.56'2 21; aa05 01-25—dc01   00-068564

Cover design by Jeanne Hogle
Book design by Lisa Hollander with Susan Macleod

Workman books are available at special discounts when purchased in bulk for premiums and sales promotions as well as
for fund-raising or educational use. Special editions or book excerpts can also be created to specification.
For details, contact the Special Sales Director at the address below.

Workman Publishing Company, Inc., 708 Broadway, New York, NY 10003-9555
www.workman.com

Manufactured in Belgium
First printing March 2001
10 9 8 7 6 5 4 3 2 1

Why not start at the beginning?

As a mother of four, over the years I've found myself answering a lot of questions about reproduction. I've always tried to respond to my children's queries honestly and made sure to start at the beginning. For me, talking to a six-year-old about how life begins is easy. Children of that age are curious, open, and not a bit embarrassed by the topic. But after years of silence, talking to a teenager about the same subject can be difficult for both the parents and the child. At least I found it so when my parents broached the subject with me for the first time when I was thirteen. So, with my children, I chose the easy route. In our household, sex is a subject that's always open for discussion, and as the questions get tougher, I want to be the one to help them find the right answers.

If your child asks about two dragonflies that are flying around linked together, go ahead and take the plunge and tell her that the dragonflies are making dragonfly babies. Every life starts the same way. What a simple way to begin the discussion.

I hope that by reading *First Comes Love* with you, your children will learn that your door is always open for their questions. And remember, "Birds do it, bees do it, even educated fleas do it. Let's do it. Let's fall in love." Thank you, Cole Porter.

—JENNIFER DAVIS

Millions of babies are born every day.

Do they all get here the very same way?

How do parents make a baby grow?

Just turn the page if you'd like to know.

About 2,400,000 human babies are born every day, which is almost 100,000 an hour. There are over one million named species in the animal kingdom, so it is hard to even imagine how many baby critters are born each day.

Love starts as a twinkle in two people's eyes,

Warming the hearts of both gals and guys.

Animals, too, feel this wild attraction,

It makes the males spring into action.

Once they've picked a special sweetheart,

Then dazzling displays of affection start.

In most species it's the male who tries to attract a female. Some show off their brilliant colors, others their sweet voice, their irresistible scent, or their graceful motion, and some are known to bring gifts.

A male octopus captivates

The interest of intended mates

By changing into shimmering stripes,

Which pleases even the shyest types.

Thrilled by his enthusiasm,

These leggy ladies just have to have him.

Most octopuses are a neutral color so they can blend into their habitat.
But when a male sees a female he likes, shimmering stripes appear on his
skin and two fleshy knobs sprout from the top of his head.

This is a fellow who carries a torch.

You might have seen him from your porch.

When the firefly is in a flirting mode,

He scribbles and blinks a special code.

The dark night sky is sprinkled with gold

Whenever he searches for a gal to hold.

Each species of firefly (which are also known as "lightning bugs") has its own blinking language. To find one of their own kind, fireflies blink a special series of flashes to each other during the courting season.

A smitten peacock shakes his tail all around.

His fabulous feathers are world renowned.

He calls to his lover as he flies through the air,

His peahen swoons for this fellow with flair.

A male peacock raises his magnificent tail feathers to attract the attention of a female (which is called a "peahen"). He calls to her, taps his feet, rattles his fabulous plumes, and, in full regalia, leaps through the air.

Even the most unpolished possum

Knows how to make love blossom.

His love call sounds a clickity clack,

It's a surefire possum aphrodisiac.

Before he prowls, he slicks his hair into place—

Who could say no to such a winning face?

When a male possum goes courting, he makes a metallic clicking sound. He also marks his territory by licking a surface like a tree trunk and then rubbing his head against the wet place, which slicks his fur back.

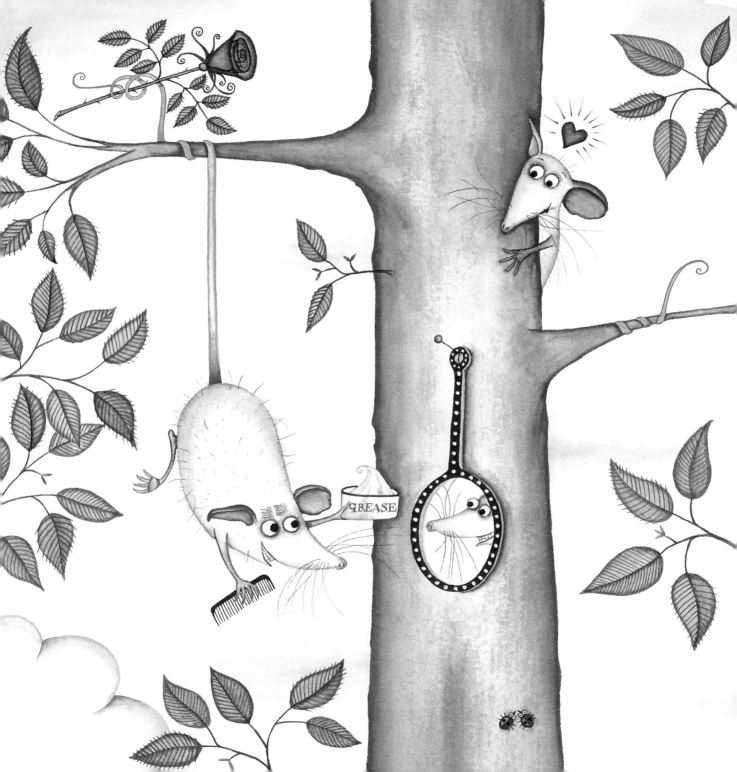

The manners of a gator may be unrefined,

But a more amorous suitor is hard to find.

He crawls for days in passionate pursuit

Of the long-tailed lady he finds so cute,

Calling to her with a resounding bellow

Till she's enthralled with this slippery fellow.

He then tickles her chin to make her swoon,

Under the still waters of the murky lagoon.

The male alligator follows his intended everywhere, all the while bellowing a loud love call. Once they slip into the water, he swishes his tail to send bubbles under her chin.

There are lots of ways that you can tell

When people fall under the loving spell.

Their eyes are bright and they walk with a bounce,

And they're extremely happy by all accounts.

They snuggle and nuzzle and smooch and woo.

Beware! Someday it will happen to you.

When people first fall in love, their body chemistry changes. Their pupils dilate, so that their eyes sparkle; their hearts pump harder, making their cheeks rosy; and their bodies release oil, making their skin glow and their hair shiny.

Creatures mate so they can give birth

And continue their species on this Earth.

A pair can mate during the night or day.

All over the world it's done the same way:

Millions of sperm are released by the males,

And off they race by swishing their tails.

They reach tiny eggs that only females bear,

Then the egg and a sperm join as a pair.

Once a month a woman releases one egg about this · size. A man makes billions of sperm, and he can produce them anytime, but it takes only one sperm to fertilize an egg. Once the sperm and egg join together, the combination is called an embryo.

Even the most delicate dragonfly

Mates in order to multiply.

Two hook together while flying around

In big loopy circles above the ground.

To mate they join in the shape of a heart,

Then off to lay eggs on the water they dart.

After dragonflies perform their mating dance, the female deposits her
eggs (as many as 700) on the surface of a stream or pond. The eggs
then spin out tiny threads, anchoring them to the bottom.

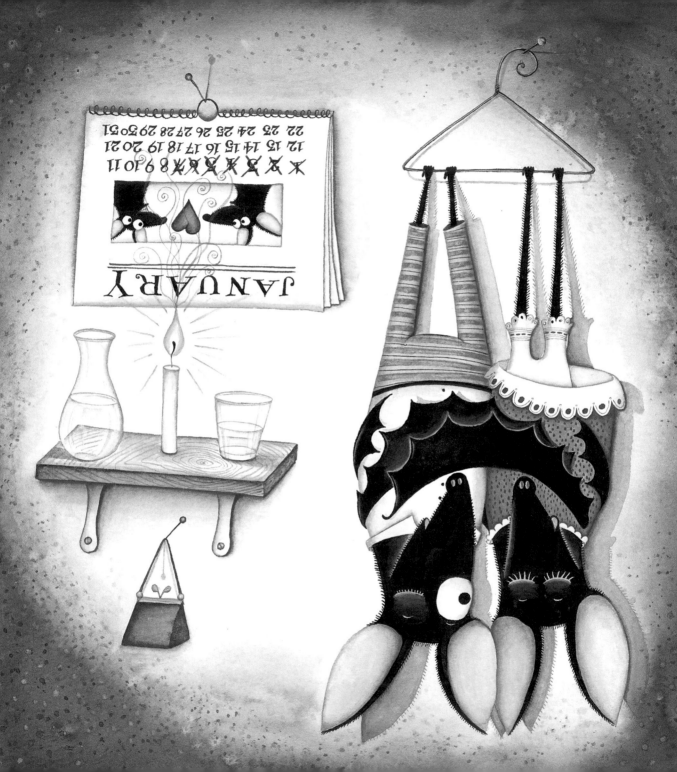

Hanging in caves by the tips of their toes,

Through long winter months bats mate and doze.

After their lovemaking, it is sometimes the case

That they sleep for weeks in each other's

embrace.

Bats sleep hanging upside down and mate that way, too. During the winter, bat couples sometimes fall asleep after their lovemaking and spend the rest of the hibernating season snuggled together.

The she-crab wiggles out of her shell

To mate with her "Jimmy" for a short spell.

For a few days after, he'll stand guard,

While her new shell grows nice and hard.

He won't leave her without her armor,

For fear a creature could come and harm her.

When a female blue crab sheds her shell to mate, her skin is soft and pink. For the few days before her shell grows back, a male crab, called a "Jimmy," protects her from fish that might want to eat her.

A penguin sings with open arms,

Enchanting his darling with his marvelous charms.

Quivering and caressing with flippers and beaks,

They touch and talk for a full two weeks.

Once they've proved their pledge of devotion,

They mate on the surface of the frozen ocean.

Penguins try to reconnect with the same mate year after year. At mating time, many penguins crowd together. In order to find each other, they sing out, and their mates recognize them by their voice.

Once people are adults and fully mature,

And know without doubt that their love

   will endure,

It's babies some couples dream of creating.

To make this happen they begin mating.

Your mother and father got this notion, too,

They wanted a baby, and it was . . . guess who?

Men's and women's bodies are made to fit together. The man puts his penis into a woman's vagina and releases his sperm near her egg.

After the mating has taken place,

The embryo is stored in a safe space.

If you're a spider, chick, turtle, or crow,

Inside an eggshell is where you'll grow.

But if you're a fox or a cat or a caribou,

Or a person just like me or you,

Inside mom's womb is the place to be,

Until you are born for the world to see.

It takes human babies about nine months to develop before they are born, while it takes a chicken three weeks. A chipmunk takes one month; a cheetah, three months; a hippo, eight months; a walrus, fifteen months; and an elephant, eighteen months.

When a lioness needs to leave her litter,

She never thinks of calling a sitter,

Because mama lions from the same pride

Care for their cubs side by side.

These lion sisters count on each other

To share the duties of a mother.

They nurse and protect their little ones

And bring up spunky daughters and sons.

 Lionesses in the same pride, or family group, take care of each other's cubs. Boy and girl cubs look alike. Male lion cubs don't grow manes, just as boys don't grow beards, until they are approaching adulthood.

Mosquitoes lay eggs that form a tiny raft,

Clumped together both forward and aft.

After these little biting bugs hatch,

Under the water goes the whole batch.

There they grow bigger for a few days,

Before flying off to go their own ways.

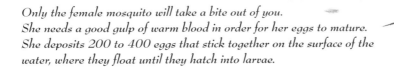

Only the female mosquito will take a bite out of you.
She needs a good gulp of warm blood in order for her eggs to mature.
She deposits 200 to 400 eggs that stick together on the surface of the
water, where they float until they hatch into larvae.

Kangaroo newborns are rarely seen

Because they're no bigger than a lima bean.

From between Mom's legs to her pouch

   they creep,

Crossing her big belly, where the fuzz is deep.

They search for milk in her fur-lined pocket

Because that's the place where kangas stock it.

In her cozy pouch "Baby Joey" will stay

Until he is big enough to go his own way.

A newborn kangaroo, called a "Joey," stays in his mother's pouch for three months. After that he ventures in and out for another five to seven months. Before he is a year old, he leaves the pouch for good.

After most spiderlings hatch from their shell,

They bid their siblings a fond farewell

And reel way out on a long silky thread

Till the wind gives a puff—then off they head.

Into the air these young ones are hurled

To begin a new life in the big wide world.

Most spiderlings are so light that they can do something called "ballooning."
They reel out a long thread and let the wind pick them up and carry them away.
Some spiders have ballooned three miles high, and others have traveled more
than 100 miles.

Can a daddy give birth to his own creation?

"No!" we all answer without hesitation.

But yes, one can, and here is a clue:

He lives in the sea where it's deep, dark, and blue.

A guy who births babies is rare, of course,

But it's no trouble for "Big Daddy" seahorse.

The female seahorse puts her eggs into a pouch on the male's belly.
He fertilizes them and grows them until the hundred or more babies
are ready to be born.

For nine months after they mate,

Parents of children wait and wait.

In Mom's womb their baby grows,

Developing hair and eyes and feet and toes.

Newborn babies can't do much on their own—

They can't eat or walk or talk on the phone—

But every parent is sure their creation

Is without doubt a tremendous sensation.

Human babies are usually born headfirst and come out through their mother's vagina.

Millions of babies are born every day,

And they each got their start the very

same way.

Next time you see a baby that's new,

Remember she got here just like you.

Even though we all get here the same way, no two people or two animals are exactly alike. No two human babies have the same fingerprints. No two giraffes have the same spots. No two zebras have the same stripes.